How to Save the Planet

Emily Bunny

We live on planet Earth,
it's a very nice place.

Unfortunately there is
nowhere else suitable to
live in space.

That's why we must not destroy our earth.

We should reduce our plastic and buy things with worth.

There's a simple saying to help you reduce your impact.

We must
Reduce, Reuse and Recycle,
that's a fact!

One little straw may seem like fun, but the problem is a very big one.

500 million straws are
used every day,
lots end up in the ocean
when they are thrown
away.

A plastic bottle holds the liquid soap from the shop, but if you buy solid soap in a bar that plastic waste can stop!

The world needs oxygen, but where can you start?

You can help by growing a plant!

Eating meat is bad for the environment too, one of the reasons is pollution from all of the animals poo.

Cows eat 16lb of vegetation to produce 1lb of meat, 2500 gallons of water for one 1lb of meat but it only takes 25 gallons of water to produce 1lb of wheat.

If you see litter, pick it up and put it in the bin.

Litter can be dangerous if an animal eats it or gets tangled in.

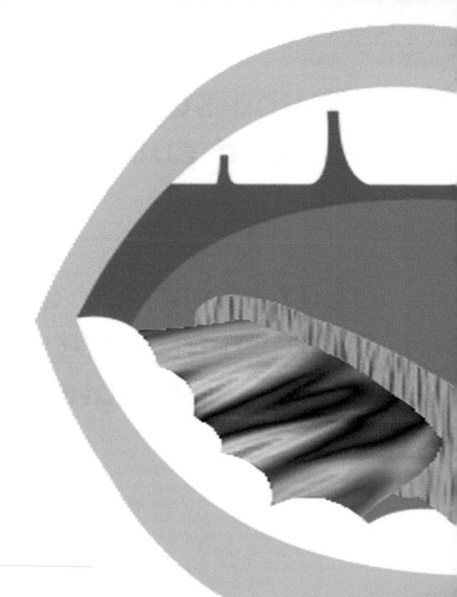

Toothbrushes are
important but they
create lots of waste too.

Instead of a plastic toothbrush, try a toothbrush made of bamboo.

That plastic bottle
might sit for 450 years
at the bottom of the
sea bed.

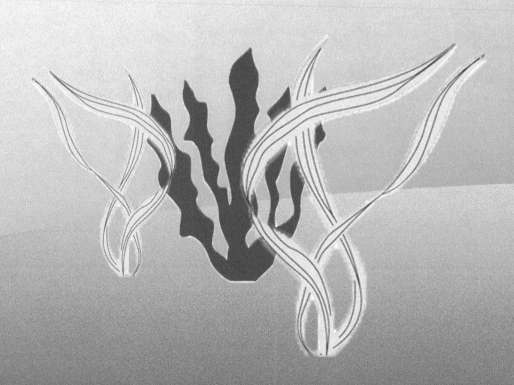

A refillable stainless steel bottle can be used instead!

Why use tin foil or cling film when it gets thrown in the bin?

Instead use a wet bag for your sandwich or keep food in a tin.

Bees are very important,
they pollinate food crops
for us to eat.

Avoid pesticides and grow
things like lavender where
bees can get nectar, which
is lovely and sweet.

Disposable wet wipes might be useful for you,

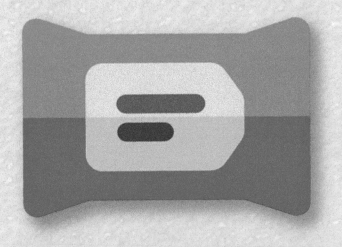

But washable fabric
wipes are just as
good too.

When you use sun cream, make sure it's reef safe.

Ensure the sun
cream is made from
zinc oxide or a
mineral base.

Any waste that you can't prevent...

Try to recycle or compost it instead.

If everyone followed
this easy advice...

Our planet Earth could
be really nice!